Voices from the High School

written by by Peter Dee
concept by John B. Welch

Single copies of plays are sold for reading purposes only. The copying or duplicating of a play, or any part of play, by hand or by any other process, is an infringement of the copyright. Such infringement will be vigorously prosecuted.

Baker's Plays
P.O. Box 699222
Quincy, MA 02269-9222

Western States
Representative
Samuel French, Inc.
7623 Sunset Blvd.
Hollywood CA 90046

Canadian
Representative
Samuel French, Ltd.
100 Lombard St., Lower Level
Toronto, M5C 1M3 Canada

NOTICE

This book is offered for sale at the price quoted only on the understanding that, if any additional copies of the whole or any part are necessary for its production, such additional copies will be purchased. The attention of all purchasers is directed to the following: This work is protected under the copyright laws of the United States of America, in the British Empire, including the Dominion of Canada, and all other countries adhering to the Universal Copyright Convention. Violations of the Copyright Law are punishable by fine or imprisonment, or both. The copying or duplication of this work or any part of this work, by hand or by any process, is an infringement of the copyright and will be vigorously prosecuted.

This play may not be produced by amateurs or professionals for public or private performance without first submitting application for performing rights. Royalties are due on all performances whether for charity or gain, or whether admission is charged or not. Since performance of this play without the payment of the royalty fee renders anybody participating liable to severe penalties imposed by the law, anybody acting in this play should be sure, before doing so, that the royalty fee has been paid. Professional rights, reading rights, radio broadcasting, television and all mechanical rights, etc. are strictly reserved. Particular emphasis is placed on amateur or professional readings, permission and terms for which must be secured in writing from Baker's Plays. Application for performing rights should be made directly to BAKER'S PLAYS, PO Box 699222, Quincy, MA 02269-9222.

No one shall commit or authorize any act or omission by which the copyright of, or the right to copyright, this play may be impaired.

No one shall make any changes in this play for the purpose of production.

Publication of this play does not imply availability for performance. Both amateurs and professionals considering a production are strongly advised in their own interest to apply to Baker's Plays for written permission before starting rehearsals, advertising, or booking a theatre.

Whenever the play is produced, the author's name must be carried in all publicity, advertising and programs. Also, the following notice must appear on all printed programs, "Produced by special arrangement with Baker's Plays."

Amateur royalty (production fee) for VOICES FROM THE HIGH SCHOOL is $40.00 for the first performance and $40.00 for each performance thereafter, subject to change, payable one week in advance of the production. Consult Baker Catalogue for current royalty information.

Copyright © 1982 By Peter Dee

Made in U.S.A.
All rights reserved.

VOICES FROM THE HIGH SCHOOL

Dedication

To Stephen, Andrea, and Stewart,
three teenagers, for their
advice, inspiration and support.

Other Published plays by Peter Dee

One More Waltz With Molly O'Flynn
A Devil In The Grass
Daughter Of A Traveling Lady
The Man Who Stayed By His Negative
No One Wants To Know
A Sea Of White Horses
Mores

Voices from the High School is performed by a group of students.

Characters and Scenes within group:
 Jean and Kevin
 Stephen and Sheila
 Doug and Ann
 Hank and Charlie
 Kim and Miko
 Andrea and Chris
 Senior Girl and Freshman Girl
 Rosa and Maria
 Harry and Jerry
 Larry and Bobby
 Ellen
 Teddy and Danny
 Millie and Carol
 Valentine's Day
 Jimmy
 Patti and Bo
 Teen Santa
 Leotard

Voices from the High School was given its World Premiere at the Boston University Theatre Institute, Boston, MA.

FOREWORD

The greatest potential of theatre is the communication of truths. Too often, secondary school actors and directors are not given the opportunity to participate in realistic, contemporary teen theatre due to the hard-nosed fact that too few plays are written expressly for them. Baker's Plays commissioned New Dramatists and Circle Rep playwright Peter Dee to write *Voices from the High School* so that the teen actor might find the opportunity to share with his fellow students, his parents, teachers and administrators, the joys and difficulties of being forced to grow up too fast in America.

Judy Klemesrud of the *New York Times* writes of this play: "This is not the usual high school pap". Yes, some of the vignettes are devastatingly honest. They might prove too controversial for some administrators and teachers (each scene was developed from the standpoint of the teen in modern America). If the producing director should find such scenes disturbing to the community, we can grant permission to omit such scenes without written request. We cannot, however, grant you permission to include additional materials from other sources. There shall be no reduction in production fee for such omission, but a special quote will be issued if a presentation in one-act form is planned.

This play can be easily produced (and rehearsed) as it calls for flexible, open staging with a flexible cast. One might choose to produce *Voices from the*

High School with a cast of ten or, as the Boston University Theatre Institute did, with a cast of twenty-five. One might also choose to add original music or use instead, contemporary, popular music. The setting might be elaborate, with platforms, turntables, etc., or a simple barestage with pieces. The important element in production is the "voice" of the play. It represents the laugh and the cry of someone desperately wanted to be listened to. The power of truth is a thing of awesome responsibility; it gives us hope, changes lives, it lives in a place within us, forever. *Voices from the High School* requires a commitment to this truth, and a desire to share it with one's fellows.

John B. Welch

VOICES FROM THE
HIGH SCHOOL

Lights up to reveal a group of high school students. A member of the group moves forward and speaks.

GROUP MEMBER. What you see before you is an amazing collection of muscles... (*Group does poses*) Sounds... (*Group does sounds*) Brain power, feelings, hearts and emotions. The high school teenage body is a universe still in the primitive stages of exploration. You can explore alone but it takes a lot of will power to be private; there are constant assaults. (*Group does loud noises and movements*) Who wants to be private anyway?

(*TWO MEMBERS of the group move out and become: "JEAN and KEVIN." JEAN enters from one direction loving the music on her Sony Walkman. KEVIN enters from the opposite direction loving the music on his Sony Walkman. They meet in the center of area and have the following exchange of words as they move to their music or whatever*)

JEAN. Kevin.
KEVIN. Jean.
JEAN. How are yah?

KEVIN. Sony Walkman.

JEAN. Great.

KEVIN. How are yah doing?

JEAN. Me too.

KEVIN. Yesterday.

JEAN. Not yet but I hear it's fantastic.

KEVIN. When did you get yours?

JEAN. Designer Jeans too.

KEVIN. How come you're just using it now?

JEAN. Oh God, that guitar!

KEVIN. "Punks And Thugs At Lincoln Center."

JEAN. On your Sony Walkman already?

KEVIN. Fabulous.

JEAN. They got it so soon?

KEVIN. How are yah doing?

JEAN. Thursday.

KEVIN. Yeah, but I'm okay now.

JEAN. A leather jacket and roach clip Mick Jagger used.

KEVIN. And on top of that; Chopin!

JEAN. It's hard to walk in a straight line.

KEVIN. Just after I blew up and told them they were out of it completely.

JEAN. I'm really not hungry, but thanks anyway.

KEVIN. Next present I open is this. I felt like a creep.

JEAN. Yogurt and a tab so I'm really not hungry.

KEVIN. I never heard of them. Any good?

JEAN. Same to you.

KEVIN. Yeah...as a matter of fact I think I even see better.

JEAN. Last year. Last year I got this sweater.

KEVIN. No. I'm hot with this music.

JEAN. Algebra class.

KEVIN. Where are you going?

JEAN. You're not in my class.

KEVIN. French.

JEAN. I got to run. I'm late.

KEVIN. What are you listening to? (*JEAN runs off to her class,* KEVIN *is slightly shocked to be so abruptly deserted. He turns and stands watching her run off*)

KEVIN. Is it that bad? (*There is a tremendous screeching of brakes, which the audience hears but not Kevin.* KEVIN *stands where he is watching Jean. When he turns and starts walking he comes to a sudden stop as he mimes walking into the front grill of a truck. He looks up, waves at the driver and gets out of the way. Lights fade slightly and the "Jean and Kevin" actors rejoin group. Lights up on another* GROUP MEMBER)

GROUP MEMBER. There are certain things it's not right to do to each other. It's like our code of justice in a way but unspoken. Like you've heard how when a chicken is wounded or weak all the other chickens peck at it. Well that's not really permitted with us. Sure, we make jokes about who's got rotten breath or sweats through their dungarees or whose got a nose the size of a blimp, but not to their face. It stinks to put another kid on the spot. They could do it to you.

(*Two members of the group move out and become:* "STEPHEN *and* SHEILA." *They appear to be sitting on a bench or wall somewhere outside the vicinity of a high school*)

STEPHEN. Coming new into this school isn't easy. If they don't know you here they can kill you. Like the first day I arrived I was wearing the wrong kind of jacket. Man, I couldn't have picked a worse one. I like how it looked on me in the store. I like material that shines. So I see this one kid staring at me and this leads to other kids seeing me looking at him staring and so I say; "Something bothering you, faggot?" And lucky for me I won the fight.

SHEILA. Did you hurt him?

STEPHEN. I don't know. I went crazy when I thought he bloodied my nose.

SHEILA. Did he?

STEPHEN. A little.

SHEILA. Like animals.

STEPHEN. Girls don't have to fight.

SHEILA. Oh yeah.

STEPHEN. Not like the guys.

SHEILA. Worse.

STEPHEN. In school here?

SHEILA. I don't care if any one likes me in this school. Being new doesn't bother me. You don't have to be nice. I don't care.

STEPHEN. They beat you up?

SHEILA. Look, I don't need a protector.

STEPHEN. Who beat you up?

SHEILA. No one!

STEPHEN. You were crying.

SHEILA. I was not! Leave me alone. I didn't ask you to sit down here with me.

STEPHEN. Okay. Just give me a minute to sort of . . .drift off or they'll think *I* beat you.

SHEILA. Let them think what they want!

STEPHEN. Stop yelling, Sheila.

SHEILA. You don't know my name.

STEPHEN. It's not Sheila?

SHEILA. Yes. But I never told you.

STEPHEN. I'm Stephen. Hi.

SHEILA. I know your name.

STEPHEN. What's yours?

SHEILA. Nobody beat me up. I'm okay.

STEPHEN. I always think somebody's been punched out when I see 'em crying.

SHEILA. I wasn't crying.

STEPHEN. You got a weird eye problem then.

SHEILA. I'm okay now.

STEPHEN. Okay.

SHEILA. You can go.

STEPHEN. I am. (*Pause.*) Where you from?

SHEILA. Look...

STEPHEN. Where?

SHEILA. Small town.

STEPHEN. What made you move here? (*Silence*) Huh?

SHEILA. My father got a new job after...

STEPHEN. What?

SHEILA. Nothing.

STEPHEN. It's not a bad jungle here. Lot of concrete you know.

SHEILA. Yeah. There was a . . . pond in the middle of the town square where I lived.

STEPHEN. Sounds pretty.

SHEILA. There were three silver elephants in the middle of it.

STEPHEN. Doing what?

SHEILA. Nothing much. Where'd you live before here?

STEPHEN. I've lived here all my life.

SHEILA. You said the first day you arrived you were wearing the wrong kind of jacket.

STEPHEN. Lived in a small town like you.

SHEILA. Yeah?

STEPHEN. Um hmm.

SHEILA. Why'd your family move?

STEPHEN. Family didn't. Just me.

SHEILA. Oh.

STEPHEN. They see me as the independent type. Just an aunt and uncle anyway, not really a family.

SHEILA. Who do you live with?

STEPHEN. 'Nother aunt. You're looking better.

SHEILA. I told you I'm okay.

STEPHEN. So what's your name anyway?

SHEILA. Sheila.

STEPHEN. You got a nice smile. Do you like ice cream?

SHEILA. You do this to all the new girls in school?

STEPHEN. Nope. This weeks special is Jasmine Mocha Night.

SHEILA. I like vanilla.

STEPHEN. Come on. I'll treat.

SHEILA. No thanks.

STEPHEN. Hey, I'm loaded. I just knocked off that new guy from Jersey.

SHEILA. (*Laughs.*) You did not.

STEPHEN. Wait'll you taste their vanilla, it's the greatest. Let's go. Okay?

SHEILA. Okay. (*Lights down on "Stephen and Sheila" and they rejoin group. Light up on another* GROUP MEMBER)

GROUP MEMBER. I remember this kid last year. Came from Santa Domingo and no one talked to him for a month. Then there was this party and it turned out he played the acoustical guitar like no one here ever heard before. Now he's Carlos and I can't get him to talk to me at all. So...I'm working on learning his language. That's what you need for study; incentive.

(*Two members of the group move out and become:* "DOUG *and* ANN." ANN *is sitting by her locker studying.* DOUG *comes down the hall and stands by her*)

DOUG. Yeah. Well I'm here...I showed up. So what's the big deal?

ANN. Quiet Doug, I'm looking over my notes for the quiz.

DOUG. Look...look...study...study. Still don't have to give me dirty looks.

ANN. I'm not.

DOUG. You're not being very friendly.

ANN. We'll be in class in five minutes. You know how her quiz's are.

DOUG. Did you study last night?

ANN. Of course.

DOUG. So relax.

ANN. Did you study? Like you promised you would? Doug?

DOUG. Sure.

ANN. What's the Kansas-Nebraska Bill?

DOUG. $8.95.

ANN. You didn't study did you.

DOUG. Ann...you're too young and pretty to be acting like my mother.

ANN. You make me so mad.

DOUG. Hey.

ANN. Last night you said you'd study. You said you'd go right home and study.

DOUG. And you kissed me good night. That was great. How about a kiss good morning. (*He kisses her gently*) I studied a little bit.

ANN. Oh, Doug.

DOUG. Honest, I did.

ANN. And smoked dope again this morning.

DOUG. Hey.

ANN. "Hey" what? I could tell as soon as I saw you coming down the hall.

DOUG. You look like an orphan...crouched up against your locker like that...remember that book we had to read *"Jane Eyre"?"*

ANN. Yeah. "Orphan." Boy, thanks for the compliment.

DOUG. Well she got that guy that rode the horse pretty excited...he had a big house and everything.

ANN. And a crazy wife in the attic.

DOUG. Hey, listen, I got divorced when I was seven. I'm over it.

ANN. I'm sure she's going to want a lot of details.

DOUG. Who?

ANN. Miss Walker...on the quiz.

DOUG. She wants more than "details." She's looking for the main thrust.

ANN. Cut it out.

DOUG. I know what I'm talking about.

ANN. You guys...all you think a woman wants is ...is...

DOUG. The inside story on Andrew Jackson. Actually, I'm more interested in Rachel.

ANN. She smoked a pipe.

DOUG. Right. She and I'd of got along real fine.

ANN. Why do you smoke in the morning?

DOUG. Same reasons my father drinks coffee. I'm an addict.

ANN. Don't be funny.

DOUG. You want me to be sad? *(Fake tears)* "Annie, Annie, my life's coming apart at the seams."

ANN. You shouldn't do it. You know you shouldn't. It makes you stupid. It makes you...

DOUG. Just one light kiss.

ANN. No.

DOUG. A goodbye kiss...then I'll leave you alone forever.

ANN. Leave me alone now. Not forever. Some
time after the dope in you has worn off and you
haven't smoked another.

DOUG. When my head is on straighter you mean.

ANN. See if you want to give me a light kiss goodbye then.

DOUG. Cripe, Ann, one lousy joint on the way to
school. Everybody does it.

ANN. I don't!

DOUG. I might as well cut the class. You're right.
I don't know any of the junk she'll be asking about.

ANN. What did you do last night?

DOUG. Don't you worry about me, baby. My life is
going just fine. After leaving your lips last night, I
walked home past every temptation with my chin up
high. Had a supper my mother told me was "gonna
knock me off my feet" and it wasn't bad, watched the
old television for a short duration, jogged up to my
room and got out the old history book Abe Lincoln
style, read...put on some music...read...popped a
pill Kenny gave me...read...put on my ear phones...
stopped reading...thought about the feel of your lips
...you...turned up the music...put...did a couple
more things...then fell asleep...I guess. Hey. I got
to class on time. Give me a break.

ANN. What kind of a pill?

DOUG. Re...I don't know. I trust Kenny, he's my
friend. He took one and he's still walking. I'm going
to ask him the exact name of it. I mean he told me
but I really wasn't listening. It's dynamite.

ANN. You look like you blew up last night.

DOUG. Should I go in and flunk this mother?

ANN. Yeah.

DOUG. Okay.

ANN. Sit down with me.

DOUG. I'd love to. (*He sits down and puts his arms around her shoulder. She cuddles into him*)

ANN. We got two minutes before the bell...lean back and get a grip on the historical parts of your brain...

DOUG. I'm grippin'...

ANN. Okay. "The Kansas-Nebraska Bill centered on the controversial issues that..." (*Slow fade of light on "Doug and Ann" and they rejoin group. Lights up on* GROUP MEMBER)

GROUP MEMBER. Getting stoned isn't the only thing that alters your mind. I was over at my friend Judy's the other night and we were practicing how to kiss boys. She kissed me. I kissed her. She kissed me. I kissed her. All of a sudden she stopped and looked into my eyes and I looked back into her eyes. (*Pause*) So we went out in the kitchen and made popcorn.

(*Two members of the group move out and become:* "HANK *and* CHARLIE." *Hank and Charlie are lying in the sun in a deserted place*)

HANK. Man.
CHARLIE. What?
HANK. Huh?
CHARLIE. You said, "man."
HANK. Yeah.
CHARLIE. Nothin.
HANK. Nice layin' out here in the sun.
CHARLIE. Think anybody can see us?
HANK. Don't care.
CHARLIE. I never look at the sky much.
HANK. No?

CHARLIE. Well...I mean lying here like we are and looking at it.

HANK. It's nice.

CHARLIE. Yeah.

HANK. That cloud looks like...

CHARLIE. What?

HANK. ...a huge...

CHARLIE. ...broken heart.

HANK. Right. Hey, man, that's pretty cool. Broken heart in the sky.

CHARLIE. One time I saw Cheryl Tiegs.

HANK. In the clouds?

CHARLIE. I swear.

HANK. Down to the teeth?

CHARLIE. The shape and the hair.

HANK. You like her?

CHARLIE. She's okay.

HANK. Got her phone number?

CHARLIE. Sure.

HANK. "Hi Cheryl, this is Charlie and I saw you in the clouds." She'd probably want to meet you.

CHARLIE. Yeah.

HANK. I'm not kiddin'.

CHARLIE. What do you think of Annie Harrigan?

HANK. Nice knockers.

CHARLIE. Yeah.

HANK. That's what you like about her?

CHARLIE. And her legs.

HANK. Fat.

CHARLIE. You think?

HANK. Gross.

CHARLIE. They're not that fat.

HANK. Gross.

CHARLIE. I think she's pretty.

HANK. Sure. She's a pretty girl with nice knockers and fat legs.

CHARLIE. Would you ever...

HANK. Annie?

CHARLIE. Yeah.

HANK. No.

CHARLIE. Think anybody saw us?

HANK. Charlie.

CHARLIE. What?

HANK. What does that cloud look like to you?

CHARLIE. Crazy kind of mushroom.

HANK. You don't see the motorcycle?

CHARLIE. Motorcycle...that cloud?

HANK. Rounding a curve.

CHARLIE. Yeah. Yeah.

HANK. I'm going to buy one. Ride away.

CHARLIE. Where to?

HANK. Away from here.

CHARLIE. I'd like to get a horse.

HANK. Horse, huh?

CHARLIE. Gallop, you know.

HANK. Regular cowboy.

CHARLIE. Just think it would feel good that's all.

HANK. Motorcycle for me.

CHARLIE. When you going to get it?

HANK. After graduation.

CHARLIE. Then off to adventures huh?

HANK. All kinds of adventures.

CHARLIE. You know...what you did...I saw my sister doing to her boyfriend once.

HANK. Yeah.

CHARLIE. They didn't think anybody was home. He was sitting on the couch and...

HANK. You watched.

CHARLIE. They never saw me.

HANK. Boyfriend look happy?

CHARLIE. Oh yeah.

HANK. Don't you think it's time I looked happy?

CHARLIE. Sure no one can see us here?

HANK. Positive. My turn, okay.

CHARLIE. Okay. (*Lights fade and* "HANK *and* CHARLIE *rejoin group. Lights up on another* GROUP MEMBER)

GROUP MEMBER. Strangest thing happened the other day. I was coming out of class and I banged into Chester Morrow and he put his hands on my shoulders so I wouldn't fall. And he said "Excuse me." And I said "That's okay." And he said, "No. I'm really sorry, are you okay?" And I said, "Yeah." And then he let go of my shoulders and I watched him walk on down the hall. (*Pause*) Well...I mean...I walked into Chemistry and started setting up and Mr. Finnegan says, "Brenda, what are you doing?" And I said, "Setting up my stuff," and he says, "but you just had the class."

(*Two members of the group move out and become:* "KIM *and* MIKO." *Kim and Miko are standing holding hands*)

MIKO. So I'll see you tomorrow.

KIM. (*Holding on to her hand throughout*) Yeah.

MIKO. You going to the video games?

KIM. Huh?

MIKO. Play the video games in the candy store; are you going to?

KIM. No. (*They stare into each other's eyes*)

MIKO. So I'll see you tomorrow.

KIM. Yeah.

MIKO. Shirt collar. (*She straightens his shirt collar*)

KIM. Thanks.

MIKO. Color is nice.

KIM. Blue.

MIKO. Yeah. (*They continue to stare—KIM kisses her gently and then pulls back and they remain holding hands*)

MIKO. You like the video games?

KIM. Sure. Sometimes. No big deal. (MIKO *fluffs her hair.*)

KIM. I'll call you tonight.

MIKO. You better.

KIM. Seven O'Clock.

MIKO. Six.

KIM. When I get home. (*Pause*)

MIKO. I have to buy a notebook for science.

KIM. Me too.

MIKO. We can buy them together.

KIM. Great.

MIKO. Tomorrow?

KIM. Anytime. (*They stand looking at each other*)

MIKO. So I guess I better get going.

KIM. Yeah. (MIKO *fixes* KIM's *collar again*)

MIKO. Collar.

KIM. Yeah.

MIKO. I like blue.

KIM. What kind of a notebook are you going to buy?

MIKO. Lined paper kind.

KIM. Great.

MIKO. With a hard cover I guess.

KIM. They're great.

MIKO. What kind are you going to get?

KIM. Your choice sounds good. The same.

MIKO. Yeah. (*Pause*) When are you going to call me?

KIM. Soon as I get home.

MIKO. I'll call you too.

KIM. Great. (*Pause, they stare at each other and keep holding hands*)

MIKO. So I'll see you tomorrow.

KIM. Yeah.

MIKO. I'm going to get a notebook with a blue cover.

KIM. Nice color.

MIKO. Blue pen to match it.

KIM. Yeah

MIKO. Maybe green though.

KIM. Sounds good.

MIKO. What do you think?

KIM. I need one too.

MIKO. Really?

KIM. Yeah. We can buy them together when we get our notebooks.

MIKO. Great. (*Pause*) I need an eraser too.

KIM. So do I!

MIKO. What about a ruler?

KIM. Yep.

MIKO. We can go get all this stuff together.

KIM. I'd like that.

MIKO. So would I.

KIM. So when I call you, we'll plan the time.

MIKO. You'll call me when I get home.

KIM. You bet.

MIKO. Or I'll call you.

KIM. That'll be great.

MIKO. Do you need to get a slide rule?

KIM. I sure do.

MIKO. We're going to have a good time tomorrow.

KIM. Can't wait.

MIKO. Me either. (*Pause*) So I'll see you tomorrow.

KIM. Yeah. (*They stand looking at each other, holding hands and not moving as lights fade. Eventually they rejoin the group. Lights up on another* GROUP MEMBER)

GROUP MEMBER. Yeah there are definitely those times when the heart starts to beat a little faster. Seems like every love song was written especially for you and this person with the big influence on your otherwise cool days. You know what I mean, like when you find yourself in places you know they go to. But you're there a little earlier so you can sort of meet by "accident." Then again, sometimes you wish it never happened to you at all. (*Two members of the group move out and become:* "ANDREA *and* CHRIS." ANDREA *is waiting.* CHRIS *comes around a corner*)

ANDREA. Hi.

CHRIS. Oh...hi, Andrea.

ANDREA. Hey, you remembered my name.

CHRIS. Come on.

ANDRIA. What's my phone number?

CHRIS. What's the matter?

ANDREA. Wrong.

CHRIS. You're acting like a jackass.

ANDREA. Watch your mouth, boy. I'll break your knees. (CHRIS *laughs*) Think it's funny? You'll look funny at the next dance. Your girlfriend will have to wheel you through all the dances.

CHRIS. I like your sweater.

ANDREA. Really?

CHRIS. Yeah.

ANDREA. I'll tell the sheep.

CHRIS. How's everything going?

ANDREA. Oh boy.

CHRIS. What?

ANDREA. I can't believe you just asked "How's everything going?"

CHRIS. Well I did.

ANDREA. Fine.

CHRIS. Good.

ANDREA. I mean, man, it's going like...wow, Chris, let me think...it's going like...flowing like...blood out of a broken heart.

CHRIS. Andrea.

ANDREA. Yes?

CHRIS. Why are you acting like this?

ANDREA. How am I acting?

CHRIS. I come around the corner and you're...I don't know...you look...angry.

ANDREA. Why shouldn't I?

CHRIS. How should I know?

ANDREA. You dumped me for no good reason.

CHRIS. Whaddaya mean "dumped you?"

ANDREA. Dumped. As in when you take a lot of stuff that you used up and don't want any more and you pick it up and go to the trash can and toss it. Dumped It's a word in the English language. Do you know anything?

CHRIS. I know I'm glad I'm taking out another girl, the way you talk.

ANDREA. Be glad. Enjoy it.

CHRIS. I am.

ANDREA. She's a jerk.

CHRIS. I don't think so.

ANDREA. You're a jerk.

CHRIS. So then you're lucky to be rid of me.

ANDREA. Don't call me lucky. I'll call me lucky. Not you.

CHRIS. We didn't get married, Andrea, you know.

ANDREA. I'd never marry you.

CHRIS. Who asked yah?

ANDREA. Four nights you never called. And in the halls...you don't even smile at me anymore.

CHRIS. That's not true.

ANDREA. It is too!

CHRIS. I can't call you every night.

ANDREA. You could for two weeks. Why can't you now? I bet you're calling her every night.

CHRIS. So what if I am?

ANDREA. She's a jerk.

CHRIS. And what are you?

ANDREA. The best thing that ever happened in your stupid life.

CHRIS. That's what you think.

ANDREA. That's what I know.

CHRIS. I gotta go.

ANDREA. Yeah, I know. The jerk's waiting. So go. I haven't got a gun. Yet.

CHRIS. So long. (*He starts off*)

ANDREA. Hey, Chris.

CHRIS. (*Stops*) Yeah?

ANDREA. That picture you gave me.

CHRIS. Yeah?

ANDREA. I tore it up. Ten hundred million pieces.

CHRIS. That cost a lot of money.

ANDREA. Hurry up, your new girlfriend's waiting.

CHRIS. See yah.

ANDREA. If you're lucky.

(*Lights fade on "Andrea and Chris" they rejoin group. Lights up on another* GROUP MEMBER)

GROUP MEMBER. Radar is necessary sometimes. We make mistakes. One or two. I mean how many times in your life are you going to be growing up, out, sideways and down all at the same time? You can be dazzled when you should be disgusted and vice versa. Radar is necessary sometimes.

(*Two members of the group move out and become* "SENIOR GIRL *and* FRESHMAN GIRL.")

SENIOR. Heard you went out with Bobby Davidson last night.

FRESHMAN. Yes.

SENIOR. He likes the freshman girls.

FRESHMAN. What do you mean?

SENIOR. What I said.

FRESHMAN. Is he your boyfriend?

SENIOR. No.

FRESHMAN. Was he ever?

SENIOR. Did you have a good time with him?

FRESHMAN. Why do you want to know?

SENIOR. Every once in awhile I check up on Bobby.

FRESHMAN. Why?

SENIOR. How far did he try to go with you?

FRESHMAN. Excuse me?

SENIOR. You heard me.

FRESHMAN. None of your business.

SENIOR. Am I acting unfriendly?

FESHMAN. You're asking a lot of personal questions.

SENIOR. Sorry. Just don't make things too easy for him. (SENIOR GIRL *starts to leave*)

FRESHMAN. Wait a minute.

SENIOR. Yes?

FRESHMAN. What do you mean; "Don't make it too easy for him?"

SENIOR. I hear he's got you pretty starry eyed.

FRESHMAN. From who?

SENIOR. He picked you up at the movies last night.

FRESHMAN. What is this, the CIA?

SENIOR. Course not. It's obvious you don't need to be told any more.

FRESHMAN. About what?

SENIOR. Bobby.

FRESHMAN. He was very nice to me.

SENIOR. He's a definite charmer. To freshman girls.

FRESHMAN. I know I'm not the only one he's taken out.

SENIOR. You see yourself as the winner though.

FRESHMAN. I think you're being a little over-protective.

SENIOR. More than a little. Three weeks ago I was up all night with one of your classmates who was trying to jump out a window because of him. She felt "abandoned" you know what I mean? Especially after some of the things she'd done with him for the first time.

FRESHMAN. Who?

SENIOR. I'm not here to gossip, I'm here to advise.

FRESHMAN. How do you know what you're saying is the truth?

SENIOR. You're in a good position to find out.

FRESHMAN. I'll talk to him about this.

SENIOR. That will be very good for Bobby.

FRESHMAN. You really resent him.

SENIOR. I resent having to take care of a poor kid he's driven hysterical because he's afraid to pick on someone his own size.

FRESHMAN. Like senior girls?

SENIOR. Or his mother.

FRESHMAN. I feel pretty well "warned."

SENIOR. Good. He's out in his car now with another classmate of yours. It might be a bit of an interruption but you can warn her too.

FRESHMAN. I might do that. Whereabouts?

SENIOR. Parking lot.

FRESHMAN. Excuse me.

SENIOR. Certainly. (FRESHMAN *starts to leave as lights fade.* "SENIOR GIRL *and* FRESHMAN GIRL" *rejoin group. Lights up on another* GROUP MEMBER)

GROUP MEMBER. You know there are certain things that happen to you that you can never, never, never tell anybody. I know you know that. And I know that you also know that, if you're smart, the first person you tell it to is your best friend.

(*Two members of the group move out and become:* "ROSA *and* MARIA.")

MARIA. You said you were going to try out.

ROSA. I know.

MARIA. So come on.

ROSA. You go.

MARIA. You said you'd do it.

ROSA. I know.

MARIA. I don't want to go by myself.

ROSA. You'll make it. No problem.

MARIA. So will you. You think I won't? Is that why you're backing out of it?

ROSA. I'm not backing out.

MARIA. Yes you are. You said you'd try out with me and now you won't.

ROSA. I'm sorry.

MARIA. You got more energy than anyone in high school, I don't know what you're worried about. I want you around to inspire me.

ROSA. (*Does cheers and jumps*)

   Hey, hey, what do yah say!

   Take the ball the other way!

   Hey, hey whaddaya say,

   take the ball the other way!

(*She stops—Looks at Maria*) Okay? Inspired?

MARIA. I want you to try out with me. We'll be the most famous cheerleaders the town ever saw.

ROSA. Sign autographs?

MARIA. You bet. (*Cheers and jumps*)

   Push 'em back, push 'em back

   Way back!

   Push 'em back, push 'em back

   way back!

(*She stops*) I stink don't I.

ROSA. No! You're good.

MARIA. I stink and you know it.

ROSA. You're good, Maria. (*Pause*) You're good.

MARIA. You really think so?

ROSA. Yeah.

MARIA. Come on down and try out with me please.

ROSA. I can't.

MARIA. I never thought you'd let me down, Rosa.

ROSA. Maria.

MARIA. No. You've been teaching me cheers for weeks so we could do this. I didn't even care at first.

ROSA. You did too. Being cheerleaders was your idea.

MARIA. So what did you practice for? Huh? (*Rosa doesn't answer*) How come you learned all those cheers and taught 'em to me? You spent all this time making me better.

ROSA. You're more than "better" Maria.

MARIA. Whatever. I think it's real lousy that you're leaving me stranded like this.

ROSA. Maria, you don't need me to become a cheer-leader.

MARIA. Yes I do. You're my friend. My best friend. If you're not going to be a cheerleader I'm not going to be a cheerleader. So let's just forget it.

ROSA. I'm sorry.

MARIA. It's no big deal.

ROSA. You'll make it if you try.

MARIA. I don't want to do it without you, okay. Can we just drop it? (*Long pause*)

ROSA. I can't try out, Maria. I just can't.

MARIA. Why?

ROSA. I just can't.

MARIA. Why?

ROSA. If I tell you . . .

MARIA. What?

ROSA. You'll keep it a secret?

MARIA. What?

ROSA. If I tell you, will you promise to keep it a secret?

MARIA. I'm your friend aren't I?

ROSA. Yes.

MARIA. So what's going on? (*Pause*) Can't you tell me, Rosa?

ROSA. I'm going to have a baby.

MARIA. Rosa!

ROSA. Yes.

MARIA. My God!

ROSA. Yes.

MARIA. When?

ROSA. I don't know. Eight months I guess.

MARIA. You're sure?

ROSA. Positive.

MARIA. Wow.

ROSA. Yeah. (*Long pause*)

MARIA. Does Johnny know?

ROSA. Not yet.

MARIA. Are you scared to tell him?

ROSA. No.

MARIA. So why haven't you told him.

ROSA. I will.

MARIA. He should know.

ROSA. Yes. (*Long pause*)

MARIA. How do you feel?

ROSA. Fine.

MARIA. I mean about having the baby?

ROSA. Okay.

MARIA. You're not afraid?

ROSA. No. Not yet. A little bit.

MARIA. A baby.

ROSA. Yes.

MARIA. Growing in you.

ROSA. Stop.

MARIA. Well. . . (*Pause*) I guess you can't be a cheer-
leader now.

ROSA. I'm sorry.

MARIA. You going to stay in school?

ROSA. Sure! Why not? You think my baby's going
to have a dumb mother.

MARIA. I mean. . .when. . .you start to show.

ROSA. Show?

MARIA. Get big, Rosa.

ROSA. Oh. (*Pause*) I don't know.

MARIA. Listen, don't worry about it. You taught me
cheers, I'll bring my notes around when you can't
come to school any more. I'll be your teacher. (*She
mimics a teacher*) "Rosa, did you do your home-
work?"

ROSA. Will you?

MARIA. Sure.

ROSA. I mean if it gets to the point where I can't come to school anymore.

MARIA. You know I will.

ROSA. Thanks, Maria.

MARIA. Hey. You taught me how to cheer.

ROSA. I'm sorry, Maria.

MARIA. Don't be silly. Mama Rosa. (*They laugh*) Mama Rosa.

ROSA. Mama Rosa. (*Long pause*)

MARIA. Have you thought about not having it?

ROSA. No. (*Long pause*)

ROSA. I'll go down with you. To the gym. Would that help? If I just came and watched. Be moral support, you know. Would that help you, Maria?

MARIA. You wouldn't mind?

ROSA. I'm proud of you. I want you to be a cheer-leader.

MARIA. I'm lousy without you.

ROSA. You're good.

MARIA. You think?

ROSA. Course you're good; I taught you.

MARIA. Will you inspire me a little first?

ROSA. (*Does cheers and jumps*)

    Hey, hey, what do yah say!

    Take the ball the other way!

    Hey, hey, whaddaya say,

    take the ball the other way!

(*She stops—looks at Maria*) Okay? Inspired?

MARIA. Si, Mama Rosa.

ROSA. Let's go then. Don't want to be late. (*They start out together*)

ROSA. Remember how to pull up your left...

MARIA. (*Overlapping*) I will...I will...

ROSA. ...leg when you do that back jump and...

Lights fade on their exit. "ROSA *and* MARᶜA" *rejoin*

group. Lights up on another GROUP MEMBER)

GROUP MEMBER. The great thing about boys in high school is that they're so stupid. Seriously, it's obvious that women are going to end up running things eventually just out of sheer inertia. They're always making these "announcements" you know; like they're going to be space explorers or something like that. Their first trip should be in the void between their ears.

(Two members of the group move out and become: "HARRY *and* JERRY.")

JERRY. "To be or not to be that is the question."
HARRY. Huh?
JERRY. Shakespeare.
HARRY. What about him?
JERRY. It's the way I'm going to speak from now on.
HARRY. Like Shakespeare?
JERRY. Yes, friend Harry.
HARRY. Friend Jerry, what's the cause of this decision?
JERRY. Methinks the way we talk today too poor.
HARRY. Like how, man?
JERRY. Like that. "Like" and "You know" and... "man" and all these unconnected phrases and unfinished sentences..."you know...like...like I mean ...you know...I mean like it was...you know." That's how we talk and no one is using "words." Magical, tragical, fantastical words that sail out of our mouths in sounds and rhythms and express our thoughts trippingly on the tongue of jubilation that we have the magnificent brains to see them and to form them and to speak them.
HARRY. Where'd you get the speed?

JERRY. Jest on, oh saucy Harry, thy arrows hurt me not.

HARRY. You're straight?

JERRY. Neither drugs nor potions give me these notions.

HARRY. What then?

JERRY. The Bard of Stratford on Avon.

HARRY. Who?

JERRY. Shakespeare! Shakespeare!

HARRY. Puts me to sleep.

JERRY. "Sleep that knits up the raveled sleeve of care."

HARRY. You're bananas.

JERRY. Bananas.

HARRY. Nuts.

JERRY. Such a paucity of expression. Dost thou infer my mind's unhinging?

HARRY. Flipping.

JERRY. No, friend Harry, with your head in bubble gum heaven, my mind is likened to a ship on seventy seas the source of which is Bill's poetry.

HARRY. Bill?

JERRY. William.

HARRY. Yeah?

JERRY. Shakespeare! Shakespeare!

HARRY. You call him "Bill" now?

JERRY. He calls me. In a torrential tintinnabulation cascade of thoughts ongoing.

HARRY. And what does Bill say when he calls, man?

JERRY. Words are birds with fragile wings and swords for lords and virile kings.

HARRY. You've had a vision man?

JERRY. Yes, Harry, a vision of sentences of words of

such variety and color we'll never live long enough to say them all.

HARRY. Tough on the jaws.

JERRY. Zounds! The jaw is dying from lack of use.

HARRY. Not the way I eat pizza.

JERRY. Mortadella madness while your brain gets nothing.

HARRY. Have you read *Othello*?

JERRY. Have I read *Othello*. Have I read *Othello!*

HARRY. Okay. He was a jerk.

JERRY. Jerk! Othello!

HARRY. Yeah.

JERRY. That's all you have to say about Othello?

HARRY. Right.

JERRY. Have you ever been jealous?

HARRY. We're talking about Shakespeare, let's not get personal.

JERRY. You're my friend what do you mean "let's not get personal."

HARRY. Othello let everybody play on his head. He was a very dumb cat in my humble opinion. He dripped words like honey on occasion, sure, but in the long run he was the drip, man, he was the drip.

JERRY. You are actually calling Othello by William Shakespeare, a drip?

HARRY. Forsooth, it's the truth.

JERRY. I suppose you think Juliet's dumb too...and Romeo.

HARRY. Juliet's okay. Romeo...well...why didn't he just grab her and get something started way earlier.

JERRY. One doesn't "grab" Juliet.

HARRY. Oh yeah, man. Know what she means by "Swear not by the moon?" She means get your butt up here on the balcony if it's so hot for me.

JERRY. I think you're wrong.

HARRY. I got my opinion; you're entitled to yours.

JERRY. But Juliet is...I mean...Juliet is...

HARRY. Breathing heavy, breathing heavy.

JERRY. Well she has a lot of words to say.

HARRY. At least they're better ones than Othello's. That jerk didn't have enough smarts to see his friend double crossing him. Where'd he grow up anyway?

JERRY. Juliet's a beautiful lady.

HARRY. I'm sure. She's got to have something with all the guys jumping around her.

JERRY. (*Looks off*) "It is my lady, Oh, it is my love."

HARRY. (*He looks around*) Where, man?

JERRY.

"I am too bold, 'tis not to me she speaks.

Two of the fairest stars in all the heaven

having some business, do entreat her eyes..."

HARRY. Is that your jazz or his?

JERRY. Huh?

HARRY. Your words or Bill's?

JERRY. Uhh...Bill's.

HARRY. They sounded a little better than yours.

JERRY.

"See how she leans her cheek upon her hand!

Oh, that I were a glove upon that hand,

that I might touch that cheek!"

(HARRY *looks off to where* JERRY *has been gazing. He looks back at his friend*)

HARRY. You hot for her?

JERRY. What?

HARRY. Angela DeCarlo.

JERRY. Angela...

HARRY. Who you've been staring at for the past two minutes.

JERRY. I haven't been "staring" at her. Don't look at me like that. Angela DeCarlo's just in my English class that's all.

HARRY. That's all.

JERRY. Yeah.

HARRY. So you're hot for her?

JERRY. Hey, all we did was read some of *Romeo and Juliet* together.

HARRY. Oh. (*Pause*) Oh. (*Pause*) Oh!

JERRY. I mean...you know...like...Miss Neville... she...I mean...like...she...said anybody here... want to read Juliet and Angela raised her hand...and then...

HARRY. You broke your arm raising it the fastest when she looked around for Romeo.

JERRY. I did not break my arm.

HARRY. You're hot for her.

JERRY. Hey listen, man.

HARRY. That's why you're talking like an Elizabethan mutant. Your rap is zap cause your heart's aflap.

JERRY. Listen...like...Miss Neville just picked me ...I mean...like it was just...you know...like... chance and...

HARRY. Jerry's hot for Angela DeCarlo.

JERRY. Cool it, Harry.

HARRY. Arise, yon friends, and cheer this flipped out loon.

JERRY. Cut it out, man.

HARRY. (*Hollers out loud*) Jerry's hot for Angela DeCarlo.

JERRY. Shut up, Harry.

HARRY. (*Continuing to holler over and over with increasing volume*) Jerry's hot for Angela "Juliet" delicious DeCarlo.

JERRY. I'm gonna kill you, man.

HARRY. Jerry's hot for Juliet Angela DeCarlo delicious.

JERRY. I'm gonna...I'm gonna...

HARRY. Jerry's hot for... (*He starts singing it*)

(*Lights fade on "Harry and Jerry" and they rejoin the group. Lights up on another* GROUP MEMBER)

GROUP MEMBER. Overheard a kid say the other day; "Only reason I go to school is to get the hell away from home." I knew what she meant. There are honestly times when even the weekends seem too long. I mean when that place you live in starts turning into a pressure cooker and the streets are too empty to help you; you kind of look forward to the sound of the lockers banging, the hollering of your friends, and even the poison in the cafeteria.

(*Two members of the group move out and become:* "LARRY *and* BOBBY." LARRY *is sitting on a street corner at night by himself. Distant streetlight illuminates him. He's hugging his knees unhappily. After a moment* BOBBY *comes walking slowly into view. He stops when he sees Larry. Then advances slowly toward him*)

BOBBY. Hi, Larry.

LARRY. Oh...Bobby. Hi.

BOBBY. Hi. (*Pause*) What's up?

LARRY. Nothing.

BOBBY. Hey. (*Larry turns away from Bobby's glance*)

What happened to your face, man?

LARRY. Nothing. (*Silence*)

BOBBY. Not many cars this time of night.

LARRY. Yeah.

BOBBY. I like walking this time of night. The quiet. You know what I mean?

LARRY. Yeah.

BOBBY. My father gets...so I like to get away from the noise...for a little bit anyway, you know.

LARRY. You come from a big family.

BOBBY. Yeah. I'm famous for that if nothing else. "There was an old woman who lived in a shoe." That's Bobby's mother, look for him in there too.

LARRY. Crowded, huh?

BOBBY. Not bad. It's okay. Except my old man, you know...

LARRY. Beats you?

BOBBY. Shit no, he drinks. Drinks and yells.

LARRY. He's a drunk?

BOBBY. (*Laughs*) Yeah. He's a drunk. (*Silence*)

BOBBY. Is yours?

LARRY. Is my what?

BOBBY. Father a drunk?

LARRY. No.

BOBBY. Mine's the champ.

LARRY. Champ, huh.

BOBBY. Yeah.

LARRY. My old man doesn't drink. He...

BOBBY. What?

LARRY. Doesn't drink.

BOBBY. Who hit you? (*Pause*) Did you fall?

LARRY. No.

BOBBY. Your cheek's pretty bruised that's all.

LARRY. Don't worry about it.

BOBBY. Sorry.

LARRY. It's okay. (*Silence*)

BOBBY. I went to see Eileen Farnum in the hospital today.

LARRY. She's in the hospital?

BOBBY. Yeah.

LARRY. No kidding. What for?

BOBBY. Nothing. Just had her appendix out. Nearly burst. But they got it in time.

LARRY. Eileen Farnum.

BOBBY. Yeah.

LARRY. The pretty one with the...

BOBBY. Shiny black hair.

LARRY. Yeah. Appendix, huh?

BOBBY. Yup.

LARRY. How's she doing?

BOBBY. Fine. Except you can't make her laugh.

LARRY. Well she's probably depressed.

BOBBY. No! I mean if you make her laugh you might pop her stitches. I cracked a joke and nearly killed her. She begged me to stop. (*Pause*) It was fun. (*Pause*)

LARRY. She's in my history class.

BOBBY. Mine too.

LARRY. Right. She's smart.

BOBBY. Brilliant.

LARRY. What was the joke you told her?

BOBBY. Oh. (*He thinks*) Actually it wasn't really a joke. There was like this nurse that came in while I was with Eileen and I had some flowers that I sort of brought with me. For Eileen because of her appendix and all. So I sort of asked this nurse about the possibility of how maybe I could get something to put the flowers in, like could she maybe help me out a little and she just gives me this look and walks out. So I says to Eileen; "What's she do around here besides suck lemons?"

LARRY. That almost popped her stitches?

BOBBY. You have to see the nurse. It's like she sucks lemons on her birthday even.

LARRY. Unhappy.

BOBBY. Totally. (*Silence*)

LARRY. She'll be okay though.

BOBBY. Eileen?

LARRY. Yeah.

BOBBY. Sure. (*Pause*) She'll always be okay. (*Silence*)

LARRY. That's true.

BOBBY. What?

LARRY. That sometimes you hurt so bad that laughing hurts more than it helps.

BOBBY. What do you mean?

LARRY. Like her appendix.

BOBBY. Yeah.

LARRY. It hurt her to laugh.

BOBBY. Yeah.

LARRY. Well that's what I mean.

BOBBY. What hurts you when you laugh?

LARRY. Nothing.

BOBBY. Your face? Tonight? (*Silence*)

LARRY. Yeah.

BOBBY. How'd you hurt it?

LARRY. My old man. (*Silence*) Someday when he hits me. He's going to get a real big surprise. You know. Cause I'm going to grow up and he's not. I mean I'm going to grow stronger and he's going to get weaker. That's just nature, you know. So he's bigger than me now but he won't always be. You know what I mean, Bobby? Know what I mean?

BOBBY. Yeah.

LARRY. Right. So some day when he beats me for no good reason. I mean just because that's the only way he can get off at life and what's driving him crazy . . . on that day I'm going to beat him. Right into the ground.

BOBBY. He beats you?

LARRY. Yeah. (*He cries in pain*) Real bad. Real bad.

(The lights go down on "Larry and Bobby" and they return to the group)

(Lights come slowly up on THE GROUP *as it bands together.* THE GROUP *expands and illustrates the following words they share together)*

GROUP MEMBER. An amazing collection of muscles.

GROUP MEMBER. Still stretching out.

GROUP MEMBER. As rich in feeling as a . . .

GROUP MEMBER. Bear.

GROUP MEMBER. Flower.

GROUP MEMBER. Coyote.

GROUP MEMBER. We can turn a city into a playground.

GROUP MEMBER. And a desert to a palace.

GROUP MEMBER. We're all alive.

GROUP MEMBER. Growing.

GROUP. The teenage body is a universe still in the primitive stages of exploration.

End of Act One

ACT TWO

Lights up to reveal the group of students again. GROUP
MEMBER *steps forward and speaks.*

GROUP MEMBER. In this high school there are _____
students. Now if you add to that the number of us in
the schools in the next towns; then the cities, then
the state, country and the world: we're a force to be
contended with. (GROUP *makes forceful sounds and
movements*) Right?

GROUP. Right! (GROUP *gets wilder and wilder.*)

GROUP MEMBER. Calm down guys. (GROUP *calms
down*) Don't want the people to get the idea we got it
all by the tail. We still got a lot to learn and tons of
feelings to deal with. As terrific as we are...(GROUP
makes "Terrific" sounds or repeats the word.)
...we still have to check ourselves out every now and
then and put a little polish on our act. (*A member of
the group moves out and becomes:* "ELLEN." ELLEN
*comes forward with a vacum hose and brush which
she uses as a microphone*)

ELLEN. Hi. I clean up dirt in my house. I use to have
to do the dishes but I've graduated from that. My
mother has a chart in the kitchen listing all our tasks.
My sister never has to do diddle. But I suppose there's
got to be some breaks for being mentally retarded.
Don't get me wrong, she functions fine in society.
Everybody loves Barbie dolls. Me? I'm on the way to
becoming a major rock star. (*Sings into "mike"*)

44

Dirt, dirt, dirt,
you are gettin'
outta mah life!!!!!

(*To someone off who hollers for her to be quiet*) I
thought you wanted me to vacum! All right. (*She uses
the hose as a "Mike" again*) Clean up on temporary
hold. So. Get on with the story of your life, woman.
They had a big party last night. So today they're
destroyed and putting my cleanup off schedule. I got
better things to do on a Saturday morning. I like to get
the small stuff out of the way so I can work on my
song. Yeah, I wrote my own song. Wanna hear it?
Well I'm going to sing it anyway. (*She indicates the
group*) Here's my band and back up group. We're
known in these parts as, "The Hoodlums." Ready,
guys?

GROUP. Ready!

ELLEN. Here goes. (*She sings into her "Mike."*
GROUP *becomes a band and backup to her "act."*)*

Spring's here baby
know how I know
you pulled out your frisby
said; let's put on a show.
We went to the park
eyes all aglow
Spring's here baby
that's how I know.
You tossed your frisby to me
I tossed it back to you,
the way you caught it
put me on a rocket
toss it, toss it, toss it,

---

*No music is provided for this song. It should be cre-
ated by the company.

toss it, toss it, toss it.
Oh baby,
toss your frisby to me.
Toss it, toss it, toss it,
toss it, toss it, toss it.
Oh baby,
toss your frisby
toss your lovin' frisby
toss your frisby to me.

(*Song ends.* GROUP *settles down quietly in background again*)

ELLEN. Watch out, Deborah Harry, you're in a lot of trouble. Yeah, big party in the joint last night. Cripe, look at this place. Obviously it was full of loaded drunks. If it wasn't for my sister they'd have used the couch for an ashtray. She gets to sleep in for saving the furniture and keeping my uncle from eating the goldfish. Yeah; thought they were moving potato chips. My little brother kept stealing their beer. So he's no good this morning either. He may never be any good again. (*Sings into "Mike"*)

I lost the only audience I ever had.

(*Stops singing*)

When my father carried him up to bed he yelled at me. It's my job to watch his only son. That's what he tells people; "This is my only son."

(*Belts into "Mike"*)

I am not his only daughter
but I will put him in his grave.

(*Reacts to father's hollering at her to shut up*) Okay. Sorry, chief. Just doing my duty. It's Saturday morning folks; clean up time. (*She puts on the vacum which we hear in great volume and she sings along with it*)

Dirt, dirt, dirt,
you are gettin'
outta mah life.

(*Lights fade on "Ellen" and she rejoins the group. Lights up on another* GROUP MEMBER)

GROUP MEMBER. I really don't think it's true that
when the teachers leave school at the end of the day
they go home and put pins in little pupil dolls. I had a
girlfriend that told me that but she thought all teachers
should be like that character Kotter on TV. I told her
that teachers are as human as we are...well the
majority of 'em...and as long as they don't openly
pick favorites, put down the less gifted or compare me
to somebody else I'm willing to let them be as weird
as they want to; and when they're hot about what
they're teaching that can be pretty great too.

(*Two members of the group move out and become:*
    "TEDDY *and* DANNY." TEDDY *and* DANNY *are sit-
    ting by a railroad track. Sound of train passing
    and sound disappears.* TEDDY *has been giving the
    finger to the train as it passes. Sound fades away*)

DANNY. How come you did that?

TEDDY. What?

DANNY. Gave the train the finger.

TEDDY. Guy in the window picking his nose.

DANNY. Didn't see 'im.

TEDDY. Disgusting pig.

DANNY. Shouldn't be allowed on trains.

TEDDY. S'why I gave him the old... (*Does finger
again*)

DANNY. He see you?

TEDDY. Too busy searchin' for boogers.

DANNY. Should be arrested.

TEDDY. Have his hands cut off.

DANNY. Fingers anyway.

TEDDY. Who'd touch 'em?

DANNY. Miss Baxter. (*They laugh*) You've done it
before though.

TEDDY. What?

DANNY. It's not the first time I've seen you.

TEDDY. Seen me what?

DANNY. Give the train the finger.

TEDDY. It wakes up the travelers. They think they're going somewhere. I just remind them what it's all about.

DANNY. World is full of nose pickers.

TEDDY. Ass scratchers

DANNY. Pimple squeezers.

TEDDY. Puke pushers. (*Pause*)

DANNY. You going to college?

TEDDY. Miss Baxter says I'm going to jail.

DANNY. Are you?

TEDDY. College?

DANNY. Yeah.

TEDDY. Here comes another train. (*Train goes by TEDDY gives it the finger again. Train passes*)

DANNY. Do you believe that?

TEDDY. What?

DANNY. That old lady that stuck her tongue out at you.

TEDDY. She had warts on it.

DANNY. Looking for Snow White.

TEDDY. Has a bag full of apples.

DANNY. Sleeps with seven dwarfs.

TEDDY. Six. Dopey won't touch her.

DANNY. Looked like Miss Baxter.

TEDDY. S'why I gave her the old... (*Does finger again—they laugh*)

DANNY. My folks say I got to go. College. What are you going to do after graduation, Teddy?

TEDDY. Hop a train. Go across the old USofA like in the old movies. See all the natural wonders and toss off the nosepickers. Wave to the kids who are giving the finger.

DANNY. Come on, man, really, what are you going to do?

TEDDY. I don't know. Enjoy the Summer.

DANNY. But after that?

TEDDY. Doing an interview, Danny?

DANNY. No. (*Pause*) Just wondering that's all. I told my dad I didn't really care about college.

TEDDY. What did he say?

DANNY. He didn't care that I didn't care and that I was going.

TEDDY. You'll be swinging on the ivy covered walls.

DANNY. Tarzan of the textbooks.

TEDDY. Miss Baxter says I can get into college as a janitor.

DANNY. What does she know?

TEDDY. Says the army will teach me what it's all about.

DANNY. How come she's always picking on you?

TEDDY. Won't give her my body.

DANNY. You're one of the smartest guys in the class when you want to be.

TEDDY. Maybe I'll join the army . . . or navy. All the cash in the nation is headin' that way. I'll become an Admiral with a nuclear sub and three yachts. One for rock concerts.

DANNY. One for women.

TEDDY. One for Miss Baxter and a pack of gorillas.

DANNY. She'd be happy.

TEDDY. On her back all day eating bananas.

DANNY. Would be good for her.

TEDDY. Yeah. She deserves some time in the sun.

DANNY. You think?

TEDDY. She grabbed me by the shirt today.

DANNY. You kiddin' me?

TEDDY. Nope. She was handing back the term papers. I hung around after class and asked her how come I got an A on it. She looked at me like all of a sudden she was a prize fighter. "You deserved it," she said like a punch. "An A looks kind of sexy," I said, "Never got one before." That's when she grabbed me by my shirt. "Wake up" she said, "Stop wasting your power."

DANNY. Little Miss Baxter?

TEDDY. Today she was a tiger.

DANNY. She's really not half bad.

TEDDY. Only person in the school who's ever been interested in my future. Only person in my life actually. Too bad I didn't meet her til senior year. (*Pause*) Think she'd marry me?

DANNY. She's going steady with the library.

TEDDY. So you'll be going to college then?

DANNY. I guess. Are you serious about the army?

TEDDY. I'll try the minimum wage for awhile. Think things over. (*Pause*) Sounds like you got a good father.

DANNY. Here comes another train. (*They sit side by side giving the train the finger as it passes. Lights fade on "Teddy and Danny" and they rejoin group Lights up on another* GROUP MEMBER)

GROUP MEMBER. Ever try to follow a girl's conversation? If she's excited it's like chasing a paper in a windstorm; just when you think you got the point she's sixteen feet over your head and whirling in a spiral. And when she's down you're supposed to have full understanding of and yet not talk about stuff that has it's roots back before either one of you were born. Basketball is a big relief sometimes, ya' know.

(*Two members of the group move out and become* "MILLIE *and* CAROL")

MILLIE. What if I changed my name?

CAROL. To what?

MILLIE. How does "Cynthia" sound? "Allison?" "Crystal," maybe?

CAROL. What's wrong with Millie?

MILLIE. Boring.

CAROL. I like your name.

MILLIE. Why?

CAROL. I like the sound of it and...the energy of it ...and...

MILLIE. Energy.

CAROL. Yeah. ·

MILLIE. That seems to be a popular word nowadays. Energy.

CAROL. Drinking is weird. It's hard to have a conversation.

MILLIE. "Hortense." That's a funny name; "Hortense." Hortense, relax!

CAROL. I think Millie's a good name.

MILLIE. It stinks.

CAROL. Carol isn't such a great name. I don't care what you're complaining about.

MILLIE. I'm not complaining, I'm selecting. "Nancy." That sounds kinda tough doesn't it?

CAROL. Sounds like your nose is stuffed up. "Nancy." How about, "Paula?"

MILLIE. Sucks.

CAROL. It's not so bad "Paula," would you like another drink? It sounds okay.

MILLIE. You want another drink?

CAROL. No.

MILLIE. I do. (*Pours straight liquor in a glass —drinks*)

CAROL. I feel kinda sick.

MILLIE. You won't get sick if you don't think about it.

CAROL. I *feel* sick. I don't have to think.

MILLIE. Well then go home.

CAROL. Like this?

MILLIE. Like what? You look okay. "Hortense," relax! (*Laughs*)

CAROL. Are you drunk?

MILLIE. No. Are you?

CAROL. You tell me, you're the veteran.

MILLIE. You really never had a drink before?

CAROL. Never.

MILLIE. Never sneaked any?

CAROL. My parents don't drink.

MILLIE. Everybody's parents drink. That's how we all got born.

CAROL. When's the first time you ever had a drink?

MILLIE. Six.

CAROL Six!

MILLIE. Six. A martini.

CAROL. Come on, Millie, that's impossible.

MILLIE. A martini. That's gin and a little vermouth. And a lot of unconsciousness. Helped me with my naps she said.

CAROL. Six.

MILLIE. Six.

CAROL. Unbelievable.

MILLIE. She was big on naps.

CAROL. What was it like. . .to be drunk at six?

MILLIE. I think I cried a lot. Didn't make me very popular. It's hard to remember. "Allison." I already said that didn't I.

CAROL. Yeah.

MILLIE. "Allison's" not such a bad name.

CAROL. A little too much.

MILLIE. You think so?

CAROL. Sounds like a blonde on a soap opera.

MILLIE. Right. (*Holds up bottle*) Have some more. Come on, it'll make you feel better.

CAROL. Okay. (*She holds out her glass.* MILLIE *pours more in. They drink*)

MILLIE. "Denise."

CAROL. "Laura."

MILLIE. "Violet."

CAROL. "Willie."

MILLIE. "Willie?"

CAROL. Yeah.

MILLIE. Too similar.

CAROL. I don't know why you're changing your name.

MILLIE. My birthday's coming up. I'd like to make a new start.

CAROL. Actually change your name?

MILLIE. Why not?

CAROL. Seems like a lot of trouble.

MILLIE. What do you mean?

CAROL. All the people that know you as Will... Millie.

MILLIE. Yeah?

CAROL. What are they going to do?

MILLIE. Use the new name.

CAROL. That's not easy. I got an aunt that just changed her name. Aunt Sophie she's been all the years I've known her and suddenly she tells us her name is now "Georgette." Aunt "Georgette" we're supposed to call her now. She gets mad when we forget. It's very rough. I'm probably going to go on calling you "Millie" no matter what happens.

MILLIE. The time I was trying to stop drinking, the woman running the program was named Meg.

CAROL. You were in a program?

MILLIE. Yeah. Meg said; "Put your mind into new things. New things." How do you like that name; "Meg?"

CAROL. You couldn't stop?

MILLIE. Sure. I was a very straight girl for almost half a year.

CAROL. What...how did...

MILLIE. Who knows? Habits aren't easily broken. Naptime. I saw Meg on the street not too long ago. Pretended I didn't know her. Poor lady looked so shocked I couldn't have handled the conversation. I like to drink. Is there really something so wrong with that?

CAROL. But six years...

MILLIE. Oh who knows, maybe it was seven or eight or...five. Shall we put my mother in the electric chair? Is that what we're supposed to do? Okay she's a stupid woman. That's no news to anybody. Never was. I didn't like the things Meg was trying to make me think about my mother. "Valerie?" How do you like "Valerie?"

CAROL. Not bad. Let me think. "Vanessa."

MILLIE. "Vanessa?"

CAROL. Yeah.

MILLIE. That's a beautiful name. "Vanessa."

CAROL. You like it?

MILLIE. Yeah. I think I'm going to be "Vanessa." Starting next month.

CAROL. After you blow out the candles?

MILLIE. Huh?

CAROL. On your birthday cake.

MILLIE. Oh yeah. Right. After that I'm "Vanessa." Think you can handle it?

CAROL. I'll try. (*Lights down and "Millie and Carol" rejoin group. Lights up on another* GROUP MEMBER)

GROUP MEMBER. Sometimes I think Fourth of July is the greatest part of Summer. It's like Summer hits its peak on that day and by mid August I start getting hungry for the action of school. Maybe if

there wasn't a Fourth of July I wouldn't notice the lag.
I mean it's like Christmas and Thanksgiving and the
last football game of the season; once they're over
with everything's kind of flat for awhile. Special days
can do a number on you.

(*A member of the group moves out and becomes*:
"MARY *on Valentine's Day*")

MARY. Remember in grammar school, when we all
gave out valentines? When you'd give out twenty and
you'd get one? Happened to you too, huh? Good. Anyway I'm really glad we don't do that in high school.
There's some advantages to being sophisticated. Fourth
grade. That was the year I gave out twenty and only
got one. From Ursula Pitt who misspelled her name.
And mine. Mary Jones. That was a horrible day. I
went up on the roof when I got home and screamed at
the pigeons so I wouldn't cry. I really hate Valentine's
Day. Thank God in high school we don't have to go
through that dumb cardboard box covered with cheap
crepe paper and phony lace routine. You know, where
you put your valentines in and then later they give
them out and the pretty girls get fifty and keep walking back and forth to their seats like grinning idiots.
That time that I accidentally tripped Celeste Jord-
an with her nose in her fifteenth one and not even looking where was going, the entire class turned on me.
Said I did it on purpose. That was a lie. I *know* who I
did it to on purpose; Cassy McGuire in sixth grade
when she hollered; "Oh it's from Richie Forbes." Like
it was a big surprise to her. A big huge, overblown,
tasteless valentine that anybody with class would be
ashamed to get. She cut her knee when she went
down. So as you can see it's not a day that brings out

the best in me. Christmas I can handle and New
Years Eve is no big problem but whoever invented
Valentine's Day I'd like to smash in the mouth for the
grief it gives me. Used to give me. I'm past all that
now. Course we won't go into Prom night and all that
stupid nonsense that puts me up on the roof with the
pigeons on Spring nights I'd rather be doing something more constructive with my life. But at least in
high school Valentine's Day is no big deal. Oh sure I
see the private exchanges and hugs around the lockers but that doesn't bother me. (*A huge red lacy
heart that reads "To Mary from Roger, with love"
begins to descend from the rafters behind Mary so
that she doesn't notice it. [or, it may be pushed or
pulled on stage]*) It just reminded me of the bad days.
In high school I'm happy to be independent, beyond
all that garbage that they no longer openly foist on
us. If I ever have any power I'm going to banish
Valentine's Day parties in grammar schools because
it's very damaging to kids. Really. If I wasn't so
intelligent I could be a very bitter person about those
formative years I was on display as a loser. It's
barbaric. Think about it. (*When the valentine is level
with Mary, "ROGER" comes forward from the group
and puts his hand on the valentine as if he is carrying
it on his own*

ROGER. Mary.

MARY. (*Turning around*) Hi, Roger.

ROGER. Happy Valentine's Day.

MARY. That's for me?

ROGER. Just a little card.

MARY. Roger, it's beautiful.

ROGER. I'm glad you don't think it's silly.

MARY. Silly? A valentine.

ROGER. Some people think they're stupid.

MARY. Really? Stupid? Not me.

ROGER. I'm glad you like it.

MARY. It's the nicest one I've ever got...since the fourth grade.

ROGER. Will you go to the prom with me, Mary?

MARY. You're asking me to the prom?

ROGER. From the bottom of my valentine.

MARY. To the prom me you're asking?

ROGER. Yeah. Will you go?

MARY. Wow!

ROGER. What?

MARY. Wait'll I tell the pigeons. (*Blackout.* "MARY *and* ROGER" *rejoin group. Lights up on another* GROUP MEMBER)

GROUP MEMBER. Crazy one last night. Dream. You know, one of those super looney ones. I'm in like a... woods...forest, you know, but it felt like I was in the ocean...which was crazy because I was in a bed sensing this rosy kind of light and even though it was the form of some kind of person I could only hear it, understand, and I nearly followed it out the window and where I was having this dream was on the twenty eighth floor.

(*A member of the group moves out and becomes:* "JIMMY")

JIMMY. First thing I did was clean up my room. Hung up all the shirts on the floor. Put my socks and underwear and two T shirts in a pile by the door. Made my bed. Sheets good and tight. Not a wrinkle in the spread. Looked at all my posters. Stopped seeing them. Rubbed my autographed baseball. Went out into the hall. Stopped. Went back and got the dirty pile of clothes I left by the door. Took them to the bathroom and dropped them in the hamper. Went into my brother's bedroom. Came out of that empty room

into all the other empty rooms upstairs. No one home
in the kitchen or rest of the house. There were some
dirty glasses in the kitchen sink and three plates with
egg stains. I scrubbed them all clean and laid them in
the dishrack. I tried to look out the window over the
kitchen sink but there was too much light. I opened
the cellar door before I opened the cellar door. I
mean I could see myself doing it. I went down the
stairs. It was like going down into darkness...water
...fog...my mind had nothing to do with it any more.
I could see the axe on the wall. The hammer. The
saw. I found a piece of rope near the washing machine
And got up on a box and tied it to a pipe. Then I tied it
around my neck, I stood on the box and looked out the
window but there was no one in the street. Couldn't
see any legs passing by. I kept one leg on the box
and lowered the other one into the free air. I don't
remember kicking over the box but they tell me I did.
My brother said something felt weird when he came
into the house. If he hadn't found me when he did I'd
have been a vegetable or dead. So I'm glad he cut me
down. And though it's a little embarrassing to tell
you all this...I'm real glad I can. (*Lights fade on*
"JIMMY" *who rejoins group. Lights up on another*
GROUP MEMBER)

GROUP MEMBER. Watch us. (GROUP *performs some
of the acts this* GROUP MEMBER *describes*) We ride our
bikes like we're going to live forever. We run on
streets and highways, balance on rails of bridges and
the edge of subway platforms. Dive from the highest
rock into the lake below, swagger into unknown places
singing and shouting.

(*Two members of the group move out and become*:
"PATTI *and* BO." PATTI *is sitting in her room
doing nothing.* BO, *an older teenage boy, comes
into her room*)

Bo. Hi, Patti. (*She looks at him*) Your mother let me in.

PATTI. Uh huh.

Bo. You haven't been to school all week.

PATTI. Right.

Bo. Just thought I'd see you there.

PATTI. What's going on is that my mother called you, right.

Bo. I missed you at school.

PATTI. She called you, right.

Bo. I was coming over anyway.

PATTI. For what?

Bo. What do you think?

PATTI. I'm okay.

Bo. That's not what I hear.

PATTI. Well it's what I know. And I'm the one who ought to know, right. I don't care what my mother's been telling you.

Bo. She says you haven't eaten for too long a time.

PATTI. I'm not hungry. I don't want another person telling me I ought to eat. My mother's been in with that boring news. She's sent in my father who's not hungry either but who's chewing on automatic and now she's dragging you in.

Bo. I called up to see how you were. Your mother didn't tell me anything; the way she was talking did.

PATTI. I'm not hungry. And I'd like to be by myself if you don't mind.

Bo. For another week?

PATTI. For as long as I want.

Bo. In this room not going anywhere?

PATTI. Quit hassling me!

Bo. I'm not.

PATTI. Yes you are. (*Pause*) You are.

Bo. Can I sit down?

PATTI. Are you going to try to feed me?

Bo. No.

PATTI. Sit. (Bo *sits. They're quiet for awhile*)

Bo. So.

PATTI. What?

Bo. What have you been thinking about?

PATTI. Bo, did you come here to be stupid?

Bo. No.

PATTI. I've been trying to to think about anything.

Bo. Have you been successful?

PATTI. Bo.

Bo. So tell me.

PATT. Tell you what?

Bo. What's got you in prison up here.

PATTI. I'd think that would be obvious to you.

Bo. It happened to the rest of us too, Patti.

PATTI. The rest of you are the rest of you. I'm me and I'm working it out my own way.

Bo. How are you working it out?

PATTI. I'm not just going to cry and moan and then wipe my nose and go on like it never happened.

Bo. You think that's what we're doing?

PATTI. I don't care what any of you are doing. I'm not thinking about any of you. I can't.

Bo. What are you thinking about?

PATTI. Carbon monoxide.

Bo. Yeah?

PATTI. Surprised?

Bo. Not a bit.

PATTI. I looked it up in a dictionary. Got the definition locked in my memory now.

Bo. Tell me.

PATTI. "Carbon monoxide. Chem..." That's an abbreviation for chemical.

Bo. Got it.

PATTI. "A colorless, odorless gas, CO, formed by

the incomplete oxidation of carbon. It burns with a blue flame to form carbon dioxide, and is highly poisonous when inhaled, since it combines with the hemoglobin of the blood to the exclusion of oxygen." (*Long pause*)

Bo. Burns with a blue flame, huh?

PATTI. That's what the book says.

Bo. Weird.

PATTI. Me?

Bo. No, no...that phrase. That phrase that's all. It's just weird.

PATTI. "Burns with a blue flame?"

Bo. Yeah.

PATTI. Why?

Bo. Forget it.

PATTI. Tell me.

Bo. It's sad. We've had enough sad shit. Look at you. You can't even get out of your room.

PATTI. Tell me, Bo.

Bo. Why? So you can memorize it. Then go on starving yourself to death. What good is that going to do anybody?

PATTI. I'm not starving myself to death.

Bo. Sure you are.

PATTI. I am not! (*Silence for awhile*)

PATTI. What does "burn with a blue flame" mean to you, Bo? Tell me so that definition in my head can explode.

Bo. One time...I don't know if you knew how hard Mary studied...she was always working on extra projects and studying those books...late at night. I'd kid her sometimes...you know...just kidding about ...the fun she was missing and the goofing. But I mean she was having fun. She and Ken...

PATTI. Yeah.

Bo. But one time...this one night...when she was up reading her brains out because she was so determined to get to college...I said...When you get into college, Mary, you're going to have to read even more. And she said..."That's okay by me, Bo, I burn with a blue flame."

PATTI. She said that?

Bo. Yeah. Weird, huh.

PATTI. They were just sitting in the car. Talking like we are now. Only about life. And that carbon monoxide was coming in without any warning. "Odorless gas." Odorless gas. It's such a stinking cheat. I know you loved your sister, Bo. I know how bad you feel. I could hardly bear to look at you at the funeral. But I miss Kenny so bad I can't even...They were just on a goddamned date. I keep playing it back and I roll their windows down so the air can get in. Pardon me, lovebirds, I say; but I'm just giving you some air. Some clean air so you won't have a death that makes no sense to anybody. Bo, we've gotten so used to crazy violent deaths but not the cheating of carbon monoxide. They didn't even know they were going down and I'll never hear him laugh again. Never. He never knew how much I loved him.

Bo. Course he did.

PATTI. I keep playing it back and I roll down the windows. I mean if the windows were just rolled down a crack Bo, they'd be okay wouldn't they, Bo? Even just one window rolled down a crack with clean air coming in. Bo, Christ, he's the only one who ever talked to me and now I'll never see my brother again. (PATTI *is crying uncontrollably now,* Bo *has his arms around her and she crys against him as he comforts her*)

Bo. We're all rolling down the windows, Patti.

PATTI. I loved him so much.

Bo. I know. I know. (*Lights fade on "Patti and Bo"
They rejoin group. Lights up on another* GROUP MEM-
BER)

GROUP MEMBER. Some of us have died in worse
ways. We're not strangers to guns or knives or cars
going too fast and out of control. In a world of toys
and tempers we've had out losses too. Even natural
diseases take some of us away. But death is not really
a part of us. We're still on the other side of plans. Our
hopes are things that we'll make real. Life is all ahead
of us. We got years to go. We' re ready to work.

(*A member of the group moves out and becomes:*
"TEEN SANTA")

TEEN SANTA. I got this job to make extra money for
Christmas. Working in a big department store down-
town. The shipping room. You know, all these boxes
come in; shirts, sox, jewelry, perfume—tons of perfume and garbage like that. All coming in for the
Christmas shopping crush. So I carry stuff to the different departments, run the ticket machine sometimes
that makes the prices for all the junk. Some of the
girls from school got jobs too. Selling crap upstairs.
So we fool around. The two guys in the shipping room
are career men. They tell me corny jokes between
giving me advice on how to live. Anyway, the store
manager comes in on Christmas Eve. She's about ten
feet tall. Bigger than anybody else in the store. Looks
and talks like John Wayne used to. She's okay. So she
comes in and says, "I don't know how this happened
but we don't have a Santa Claus today. Christmas Eve
and the company hired the guy up to yesterday. Now
there's a bunch of mother's and kids out there and an
empty chair where Santa should be." Then she stands
there, her head scraping the ceiling. Old John keeps

unpacking the merchandise and Joe, the other guy,
sort of nods his head in sympathy with her as he winks
at old John and nods toward me and I'm finally
mastering the ticket machine. I got perfume prices
with the right department code flying out at a hundred
miles an hour. "So what are we going to do?" She
says again, casual; one hand on her hip, not her
holster. "Peter'd be a great Santa," says old John as
he keeps stacking up beautiful plaid Arrow shirts. She
looks me over. "He's too skinny." "Not as skinny as
Joe," says old John. "True," she answers. "You
know I'm no Santa Claus," John continues, "and
you're a little too tall." "Right," she says with a grin
and they all turn and look at me. "Wait a minute," I
say, "there's no way I'm gonna..." "Pillows," says
Joe...We'll stuff him with pillows." "Have him up on
the chair in five minutes," she says, "there's a line
building." And she turns around and rides off into the
sunset. Next thing I know nobody's listening to me and
I'm in this red suit, stuffed up with pillows and I got
this white wig on and a red hat with a bell on the end
of it and Joe and old John are laughing their heads off
and calling all the sales ladies in from the men's department, which is right outside the door, to check me
out. One of them, Mrs. Parnasus, puts my beard on
and says she hopes I won't get stuck in her chimney
that night. They give me this big red bag full of empty
boxes to throw over my shoulder and shove me out into the store. "What am I going to say to these kids?"
I'm thinking, I know they're going to pull my beard off
and stick their fingers in my eyes. I sure don't believe
I'm Santa Claus. Why should they? I'm going to be
responsible for wrecked illusions. The mothers will
probably sue the store. Well they stuck me out here,
full of pillows from the houseware department, so it's
not my fault. I'll do what I can. Off I go to my throne

which is on the landing between the two floors. I
lumber up the stairs with my big stuffed pack of
empty boxes, sit down, mutter a couple of mild ho,
ho, ho's and wait for the worst. (*Pause*) Well let me
tell you something. Everybody should be Santa Claus
once in their life. I don't think I've ever seen belief
like I did that day. I never took a break. Kid after kid
after kid comes down the stairs to me, up the stairs to
me. Fingers in their mouth, fingers in their nose,
eyes wider than anything you ever saw. Sitting on my
lap, looking up at me, hardly able to speak. Not one of
them touched my beard. My voice kept getting deeper
and deeper. A lot of them brought something for Ru-
dolph and I said he'd share with the other reindeer. I
mean I really felt like I'd just come in from the North
Pole and had a lot of traveling to do that night so none
of these heavy believers would be let down. *I* didn't
even touch my beard. So it was really great. (*Pause*)
Oh yeah though. Something did happen to bring me
back to reality. (*Pause*) See, I'd really been sitting
there a long time, over three hours, I think, in really
intense continuing raps and negotiations with a lot of
kids who knew what they wanted when they could
finally talk. So what I didn't realize was that my Santa
tummy pillows had all risen up into my chest. So when
I finally got off my throne and started downstairs to
go back to the room, I got to take about two steps when
my red pants were down around my ankles. There was
Santa Claus in his underpants and skinny legs standing in the middle of his hometown department store
with the whole town doing last minute shopping. Talked about wrecked illusions. I reached down and grabbed my pants back up, held on to them and my falling
pillows and ran as fast as I could to the shipping room.
I couldn't help it that my big red bag of empty boxes
kept banging customers on the head as I made tracks.

So if you hear about a legendary Santa Claus strip;
relax it was only me. (*As lights fade on "Teen Santa"
the* GROUP *leaves the stage until only one is left in a
pool of light*)

GROUP MEMBER.*

> Memory is an empty house
> we've yet to see or buy
> for furniture we've nothing;
> a song, a joke, a sigh.
> Within the dance of shadows
> we bring the light of laughter
> a thousand suns are in us
> to illuminate the drifter.
> Rhythm takes us everywhere
> our ears are still not deaf
> we'll walk barefoot into history
> and never lose our breath.

(*As group member leaves another group member
returns as* HECTOR *dressed in a "Leotard"*)

(HECTOR *starts working out.* FELIX *enters*)

FELIX. What the hell have you got on?
HECTOR. A leotard.
FELIX. Leotard?
HECTOR. Leotard.
FELIX. Looks faggoty.
HECTOR. It's for dance class.
FELIX. You're in that class?
HECTOR. That's why I'm in the leotard, baby.
FELIX. Gonna start wearing an earring?
HECTOR. I don't need that for dancing.
FELIX. I got football practice. I'll see you later.

*Note: In the premiere production, this poem was set
to music and sung. Original music may be created
if you wish.

HECTOR. See yah, Felix.

FELIX. (*As he goes*) Don't pop out of your tights.

HECTOR. Leotard. (*He practices some dance steps and stretches.* FREDDY *enters eating a big messy sundae. He watches Hector*)

FREDDY. What are you doing, Hector?

HECTOR. Dancing, man.

FREDDY. Some outfit you got on.

HECTOR. You ought to get one.

FREDDY. No way.

HECTOR. Be good for you, Freddy.

FREDDY. They'd have to knit six of those things together and I'd still get arrested for indecent exposure. (HECTOR *keeps moving in dance steps and stretches*)

FREDDY. Want some ice cream?

HECTOR. Not right now.

FREDDY. I couldn't live without ice cream (*He watches Hector and eats ice cream*) Is there a dance class here or something?

HECTOR. Yeah.

FREDDY. Where's everyone else? Trying to get into the uniform? (*He laughs with great joy at his joke and eats*) Chocolate-Chocolate Chip is the answer to everything. Everything. (*He watches* HECTOR *dance*) You the only one in the class?

HECTOR. I'm early.

FREDDY. Like it a lot, huh?

HECTOR. You got it, Freddy.

FREDDY. I'm losing weight just watching you, man.

HECTOR. That's what you think.

FREDDY. Well I gotta go. I told Annie I'd meet her at the Pizza Hut.

HECTOR. Take it easy, Freddy.

FREDDY. You too. (*As he leaves*) Don't split your hotdog skin.

HECTOR. Leotard. (*Alone continues practicing and dancing.* SUSIE *enters and watches him for awhile*)

SUSIE. Hey, Hector.

HECTOR. Hello, Susie.

SUSIE. You look great in the leotard, man.

HECTOR. Thanks.

SUSIE. It really turns me on.

HECTOR. Stay and watch us dance, you'll really get turned on.

SUSIE. Don't have the time. See *you* later.

HECTOR. Bye. (SUSIE *goes* HECTOR *continues to practice by himself.* CATHERINE *enters with a bag*)

CATHERINE. Hi, Hector.

HECTOR. Hi, Catherine.

CATHERINE. You're always here first.

HECTOR. You're always here second.

CATHERINE. How are you today?

HECTOR. Fine.

CATHERINE. Good.

HECTOR. How are you?

CATHERINE. Eager for the workout.

HECTOR. Me too. (*He continues to warm up and move.* CATHERINE *takes off her coat. Then she takes off her outside clothes until she is also in a leotard. She sits down and takes off her street shoes and puts on her dance shoes. As she switches shoes she speaks.* HECTOR *keeps dancing*)

CATHERINE. My grandmother says she's waiting to see our first show.

(*Music begins*)

CATHERINE. I say to her; "Oh that's years away." She laughs and says, "What are years to me now? Time is only slow to you. Before you know it," she says, "there I'll be in the front row and there you'll be . . . up on the stage." She used to dance you know.

HECTOR. She did? (*Never stops his movement*)

CATHERINE. Yes. In Spain.

HECTOR. What kind?

CATHERINE. Flamenco.

HECTOR. Anything else?

CATHERINE. Ballet. Mrs. Kernansky, she lives next door. My grandmother's friend. Used to dance too. They're always showing me pictures. "All the famous dancers," they say over and over as if they think I'm never listening to them, "had to work very hard." It's not work ladies, I say to them, it's fun. They laugh when I say that. They know I'm hooked. (*She moves into the area where Hector is and exercises and moves. HECTOR and CATHERINE no longer speak. They move to their exercise and the music we now hear and they imagine. All the rest of the group, in leotards, come in and join their movement. They dance until the fade out of light and music.*)

END

TWAIN BY THE TALE!

A Two Act Revue
of Mark Twain Stories,
Sketches and Monologues

by DENNIS SNEE

The unpredictable wit and timeless perceptions of America's greatest humourist are brought to life and celebrated in this brilliantly composed revue. Twain's unsurpassed talent for documenting the chronic, and comic, weaknesses of human nature is the focus of this easily stageable show. Some targets laid bare by Twain's incisive assaults are bigots and bureaucrats, monarchs and moralists, cowardly duelists and frustrated suitors. The worldly-wise Twain's humourous and sometimes jaundiced perspectives on German fables, Italian artists, French presumptions and Irish combatants are also included. Delightfully sprinkled throughout the show are Twain's unreserved thoughts on friendship, vice, good breeding, the origin of the species, as well as appearances by the author himself. This presents an opportunity for a strong character portrayal as Twain steps into and around the onstage action, answering correspondents, interjecting his opinions, and encountering an unsuspecting interviewer in one of the most cockeyed question and answer sessions in the history of American letters. Twain once advised the news media, "The reports of my death are greatly exaggerated." Audiences as well as performers will echo that sentiment after enjoying this bright theatrical sampler of material from America's best-loved humourist.

6 men, 5 women
Open Stage

ONE-ACTS

IF IT DON'T HURT,
IT AIN'T LOVE

DRAMA

by JOHN R. CARROLL

2 Men, 2 Women
Interior

A bright young girl is dying of terminal cancer, and is surrounded by two people who love her dearly. Terrie, a charming and daffy orderly, loves her out of a kind of obligation—an acceptance of her fate. Cathy's mother is running away from the situation and is so afraid about her pending death, that she builds a wall of fear, not letting any honest emotion through. These two different masks are like the illness itself—they are both being torn from within. It is Cathy, through learning how to live and to die, who helps in the reconciliation of the two people she loves the most. This is a gallant, touching, unexpectedly humorous one-act that makes an overwhelming statement about the reality of the life cycle.

A NEW SUNRISE

COMEDY

by HERMAN COBLE

2 Men, 2 Women
Exterior

Two charming, eccentric elderly ladies arrive on the porch of the local funeral home with the intention of dying there by drinking wine laced with poison. "We thought the town could drive by in their cars to pay their respects and not have to bother about getting out. A kind of drive-in viewing." However, they become a bit tipsy before the wine has been poisoned and, through the efforts of a traveling salesman, avoid the meeting with their maker. In fact Electra and Cassandra are so taken with the young salesman, they decide to ask him to accompany them on a trip to Paris, France! About death? "Oh, to hell with that. We can die when our time comes." This is a one-act of charm, wit and great warmth.

"THE BUTLER DID IT"

A Parody on English Mystery Plays
with an American Twist
by TIM KELLY

5 Men, 5 Women—Interior

Can be Played as Farce or Humorous Satire.

Recommended for All Groups.

Miss Maple, a society dowager noted for her "imaginative" weekend parties, invites a group of detective writers to eerie Ravenswood Manor on Turkey Island, where they are to assume the personalities of their fictional characters. The hostess has arranged all sorts of amusing incidents. Everything from a mystery voice on the radio to the menacing face at the window. Secrets abound in the creepy old mansion. Why does the social secretary carry a hatbox everywhere she goes? Who's the corpse in the wine cellar? Why do the figurines keep falling from the mantel? And how about the astonishing female who arrives via helicopter during a howling storm? When an actual murder takes place, each of the guests realizes he or she is marked for death. The outraged hostess offers an immense reward to the detective who brings the killer to justice. What an assortment of zany sleuths! An inscrutable oriental, a seedy gumshoe, a scholarly clergyman, a sophisticated, dog loving New York couple, an intellectual type who idolizes Sherlock Holmes. When they're not busy tripping over clues, they trip over each other. The laughs collide with thrills and the climax is a seat-grabber as the true killer is unmasked and almost everyone turns out to be someone else.

". . . Successfully interweaves all the classic elements with an imaginative approach . . . a stylish cross between *Ten Little Indians* and *The Cat and the Canary* . . . Great fun and strictly for laughs . . ." Stewart, *Sun Valley (Ca.) Green Sheet.* "Kelly knows how to write a spiney mystery with a generous injection of wild humor . . . as good as any representation of an Agatha Christie or an Erle Stanley Gardner title would be on stage." Jarrett, *Arizona Journal.*